THIS BOOK BELONGS TO:

—·—·—·—·—·—·—·—·—·—·—·—·—·—·—·—·—·—·—

CHRISTMAS 2002

Christmas
with Southern Living
2002

Edited by Rebecca Brennan,
Julie Gunter, and Lauren Brooks

Oxmoor
House.

©2002 by Oxmoor House, Inc.
Book Division of Southern Progress Corporation
P. O. Box 2463, Birmingham, Alabama 35201

Southern Living® is a federally registered trademark belonging to
Southern Living, Inc.

ISBN: 0-8487-2522-0
ISSN: 0747-7791
Printed in the United States of America
First Printing 2002

Editor-in-Chief: Nancy Fitzpatrick Wyatt
Executive Editor: Susan Carlisle Payne
Art Director: Cynthia Rose Cooper
Copy Chief: Catherine Ritter Scholl

Christmas with Southern Living® 2002

Editor: Rebecca Brennan
Foods Editor: Julie Gunter
Associate Editor: Lauren Caswell Brooks
Editorial Assistant: Suzanne Powell
Senior Designer: Melissa M. Clark
Senior Photographer: Jim Bathie
Photographer: Brit Huckabay
Senior Photo Stylist: Kay E. Clarke
Photo Sylist: Ashley Wyatt
Illustrator: Kelly Davis
Director, Test Kitchens: Elizabeth Tyler Luckett
Assistant Director, Test Kitchens: Julie Christopher
Recipe Editor: Gayle Hays Sadler
Test Kitchens Staff: Jennifer A. Cofield; Gretchen P. Feldtman, R.D.;
    David Gallent; Ana Price Kelly; Kathleen Royal Phillips; Jan A. Smith
Publishing Systems Administrator: Rick Tucker
Director, Production and Distribution: Phillip Lee
Books Production Manager: Theresa L. Beste
Production Assistant: Faye Porter Bonner

Contributors
Copy Editor: Adrienne Short Davis
Editorial Interns: Megan Graves, McCharen Pratt
Stylist Assistants: Lauren Brasher, Cathy Mathews

Front cover: Bourbon-Chocolate Pecan Pie, page 143
Back cover, clockwise from top left: All Aglow, page 123;
    Abundantly Appealing, page 39; Toile Santa, page 170;
    Mocha-Orange Bûche de Noël, page 88

To order additional publications, call 1-800-633-4910.

For more books to enrich your life, visit **oxmoorhouse.com**

CONTENTS

WITH SOUTHERN STYLE
8

TABLETOP MAGIC
30

CASUAL HOLIDAY MEALS
48

THERE'S NO PLACE LIKE HOME
94

IT'S THE THOUGHT
126

HOLIDAY RECIPES
138

WITH SOUTHERN STYLE

Renowned for hospitality, the South is especially welcoming at Christmastime with homes resplendently attired in native greenery and natural materials.

ENCHANTING ENTRIES

Wreaths and garlands set the standard for outdoor decorating, but this year add a new twist. For example, the garland pictured here is decked out with eucalyptus branches and trimmed with twig balls, pinecones, and ribbons. Turn the page for more fresh ideas.

1 A brick facade poses no problem for hanging a garland. Using a hammer, tap masonry nails into place in the mortar part of the brickwork. Leave plenty of nail showing to allow space for the garland to hang.

2 Once the nails are in place, drape the garland over the doorway. We used two garlands to give more visual weight. For additional fullness, tuck in or wire greenery clippings to the garland.

3 Pinecones are inexpensive embellishments for garlands and wreaths. Wrap floral wire around the bottom of the cone, between the rows of petals. Twist the wire to secure, and use the ends to attach the pinecone to the garland or wreath. Use wire to attach the twig balls, as well.

4 Holiday decorating calls for loads of ribbons and bows. For a quick-and-easy bow, from a long length of ribbon, form a few big loops then twist floral wire tightly around the center. Make lots of loops for a big bow. Pull the loops toward the center to fluff the bow. Attach the bow to the garland using the wire ends.

MAGNOLIA MAGNIFICENCE

▲ Steeped in Southern lore, magnolia is the region's quintessential holiday greenery. The wreath shown uses the versatile leaf to full advantage, contrasting the glossy green top side with the rich brown of the underside. Sprigs of feathery juniper add a lacy complement. Two metal mesh cones wired to the wreath are filled with fresh flowers and holly. A variety of decorative cones can be found at import and crafts stores.

Each peak of the swagged magnolia garland is punctuated with a flower-filled cone. Filling the cones with water-soaked floral foam in heavy-duty plastic bags keeps the flowers and greenery fresh for up to a week. ▶

Metal mesh cones and ribbons are attached to the garland using floral wire. ▼

PLAIN TO FANCY

Take one evergreen wreath and add embellishments to your heart's content. We show you how to go from plain to fancy in a few easy steps.

▲ Red ribbons on a green wreath convey the essence of Christmas decoration. If you're a purist, you may prefer to stop here with your add-ons. For the ribbons featured on this wreath, make a loop with a length of ribbon, twist a short floral wire around the loop, leaving ribbon ends free. Use the wire ends to attach the loops and a bow to the wreath.

▲ For a showier wreath, make a gathering foray into your backyard. Clusters of red berries display bright color, while dried hydrangea blooms, misted with red spray paint, contribute a delicate texture to the wreath. Long pieces of grapevine and twisted strands of dried grass convey a bountiful look. A lively plaid bow nestles behind the red one.

For sparkle, red and green Christmas ornaments and a glittery gold bow are added to the wreath. Long pieces of floral wire work well to attach all the decorations. ▶

FRESH AND FRAGRANT

The heady aroma of evergreens, herbs, and florals instantly evokes thoughts of Christmas in these homes' holiday decorations. Backyard clippings and pots of favorite seasonal plants make it easy to blend natural materials with holiday finery for beautifully vibrant displays.

FIRST IMPRESSIONS

If space allows, consider placing your tree in the foyer. You'll enjoy passing it as you go about your daily business in the house, and guests will be able to appreciate one of your most outstanding decorations as soon as they enter.

SPLENDIDLY SWAGGED

A Fraser fir garland is the starting point for a mantel treatment whose elaborate looks belie its easy execution. Clusters of pepperberries tucked in among the garland's branches, a small crèche, and family heirloom cone trees are the central focus of the design.

Vases filled with cypress, juniper, and pepperberries give symmetry to the arrangement. On the coffee table, a deep red vase filled with juniper berries continues the design and complements the vases on the mantel. Water in the vases will keep the clippings fresh for about two weeks. The berries in the garland may dry out and need to be replaced after a few days, or place the stems in water vials to keep them fresh for longer. Hide the vials under the garland.

◀ AROMATIC AMBIENCE

Moss-wrapped pots of lavender impart an unconventional twist to this evergreen garland embellished with pepperberry sprays. Basketwork figures of Mary and Joseph stand at the center. A cozy fire in the fireplace will release the lavender's fragrance; however, the heat dries the natural materials. Water the lavender frequently and keep fresh pepperberries on hand to replace dried ones as needed. To be safe, always keep greenery and decorations well away from the fireplace opening.

▲ SIMPLE STYLING

A modest papier-mâché nativity scene surrounded by fresh plants and greenery animates this tabletop. Two ivy topiaries act as a lush backdrop for the figurines, and the mixed-greenery garland over the mirror elegantly frames the traditional setting. An advantage of using fresh potted plants such as ivy, rosemary, and lavender as a part of your seasonal decorations is that the plants can be enjoyed long after the holidays are over and may be called into service for the next holiday season.

A GRAND GATHERING

Rosemary topiaries and a concrete cherub flanked by metal reindeer form the foundation for this tabletop tableau. The grouping is enlivened with clippings of pine, Fraser fir, cypress, deciduous holly, and pepperberries. Greenery and berries wired to the low-hanging chandelier visually link the tabletop arrangement and lighting fixture for a strong overall impact. Look for rosemary topiaries at nurseries and home-and-garden centers beginning around Thanksgiving.

EVERLASTING CHARM

Dried flowers and grasses are used in abundance on this tree (and can be reused year after year). Feathers and dried grass stems create a fanlike tree topper. The bow hides the floral wire that holds the stems in place. Other decorations include seed and berry balls and raffia-tied bouquets of dried grass tucked among the branches. Thick, dried flower garlands complement the tree's large size.

ECLECTIC MIX

Juxtaposing elegant silver cups and candleholders with rustic pottery jugs holding seeded eucalyptus and heather showcases favored collectibles in a refreshingly individual holiday style.

DINING ROOM DRAMA

◀ Crystalline trees and silver accents bring to mind a wintry forest scene along the length of this dining table. A mix of greenery clippings unifies the grouping. Votive candles and pepperberries provide sparkle and color. In the center of the table, a silver compote holds an arrangement of potted plants and flowers. A small, water-soaked block of floral foam in the center of the compote holds the flower blooms, while the plants, in tiny plastic pots, are tucked in around the floral foam. When using silver containers for this purpose, be sure to line the bowls with plastic or with waterproof liners before adding the plants. To protect the tabletop, place the arrangement on top of a table runner.

ELEGANT AND EASY

▼ A boxwood wreath punctuated with berries encircles an ornate silver candleholder. Grazing reindeer are a whimsical touch. To protect your table, place the wreath and candleholder on a clear glass plate.

▲ HOLIDAY SETTING

Poinsettias—still in their plastic pots—are tucked into iron plant stands in the corners of this cozy sitting room. Sheet moss lining the plant stand baskets hides the pots. Note how simple touches such as the garland over the windows, the wreath, the pillows, and the silver trees mesh together for a cozy seasonal ambience.

TABLE MATTERS ▶

Set your dining table with a season-long decoration. Here, the Christmas tree-design plates determine the theme, which is reinforced with the family's collection of twig and painted trees arranged as a centerpiece. Rosemary topiaries in terra-cotta pots are a fresh (and fragrant) component, while ornament candles contribute a sparkling, festive air.

◀ OVER THE TOP

A large gathering basket, secured to the chimneypiece with hooks and wires, is overflowing with a wide variety of seasonal clippings. A block of water-soaked floral foam placed in a heavy-duty plastic bag sits inside the basket and keeps the greenery fresh for a week to ten days. Deciduous holly berries awaken the garland and the basket with cheery color.

PRETTY IN RED AND GREEN ▼

A berry-laden holly wreath, held in place with floral wire, is a jolly accent to the evergreen garland. The play of green and red is repeated on every shelf with evergreen clippings and shiny apples, and is seen again in the basket holding a rosemary topiary encircled by apples. For maximum impact, repeat decorative elements. Here, for example, evergreens and berries, apples, candles, and nutcrackers combine to strengthen the Christmassy atmosphere.

TABLETOP
MAGIC

What fun to cover every tabletop with holiday cheer!
Here, we show ways to use ordinary materials for
extraordinary seasonal centerpieces and table settings.

TASTEFULLY SET

*With an evergreen garland and charger there's no need
for a conventional centerpiece. Soak the greenery overnight before arranging,
and it will stay fresh and fragrant for three to five days.*

TRIM THE TABLE
Clippings of cedar, pine, boxwood, holly, and hypericum berries are wired
together to make this garland that is attached with corsage pins to the
tablecloth. For easy assembly of the garland, make several small bundles of
clippings, then wire the bundles together to achieve the desired length for
the garland.

DRESSED FOR DINNER

Encircling your dinner plates with fresh greenery chargers is a quick and inexpensive way to a stunning table setting. Since the greenery stays fresh for several days, the chargers can be a fragrant part of your dining room decorations.

To make the charger, hot-glue sprigs of greenery and berries around the edges of a cardboard cake round (check with the grocery store bakery for these). We spray-painted ours, but it's okay to leave it unpainted, as well. You may prefer to remove the charger when dining.

MERRY AND BRIGHT

Setting your table with Christmas china brings cheer to every meal. The table pictured here features plates with matching cups, chargers, flatware, place mats—even candles! However, you don't have to buy a complete set of matching tableware to set a festive table. You can buy salad or dessert plates with a holiday pattern, and use a white or complementary color dinner plate as a charger under the holiday plate. Accessorize with candles and glassware that you have on hand. Place greenery sprigs or berries along the center of the table, or fill a vase with fragrant pine and cedar for a centerpiece. Knot lengths of ribbon around napkins to act as napkin holders and to reinforce the color scheme.

SIMPLY GRAND

Using lots of your favorite things can produce a spectacular result. Here, a red table runner and place mats, white napkins and dinner plates, and green goblets and salad plates set the holiday mood. Silver containers and candlesticks shimmer as they reflect the Christmas tree lights. Rich red roses, berries, and lilies lend extravagance to the tabletop. Greenery sprigs tucked among the flowers define the arrangements as holiday decorations. Red candles and the wreath design on the napkins are good finishing touches. Remember to line silver containers with plastic bags or protective liners before filling them with water-soaked floral foam and flowers.

CLASSIC FOLDS

Elevate an essential part of the table setting to prominence
when you add a dash of panache to your napkin folds.

FRENCH FOLD

1. Fold the napkin in half diagonally with the fold at the bottom.

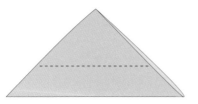

2. Fold up the bottom folded edge two-thirds toward the top point.

3. Beginning at one side of the bottom edge and working toward the other, pleat the napkin. Tuck the pleated end into a coffee cup.

NEATLY TIED

1. Fold the napkin in half diagonally with the fold at the bottom.

2. Holding the bottom folded edge at the center, fold the right and left points up toward the center point.

3. Fold the bottom point up to about one inch below the top point. Fold under the right and left sides. Tie a ribbon around the folded napkin, if desired.

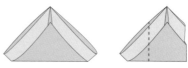

POINSETTIA POINTS

1. Fold the corners of the napkin toward the center. Then, fold the new corners toward the center.

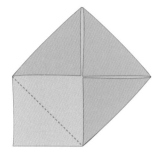

2. Turn the napkin over, keeping the center points together. Fold the corners toward the center.

3. Holding the center securely, pull the corners out and up from the underside to make the points. Place an ornament or small gift box in the center of the napkin.

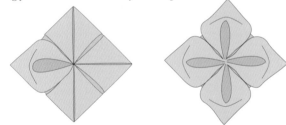

POCKET FOLD

1. Fold the napkin in quarters. Position the napkin so that the free points are at the upper left corner.

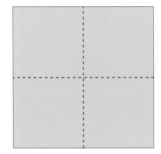

2. Fold the upper left corner of the top layer down toward the lower right corner.

3. Fold under the top right and bottom left corners. Place silverware in the pocket.

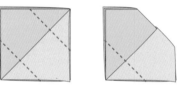

FRUIT CENTERPIECES

*An arrangement to grace the center of the table is a tribute
to the specialness of the season. This year consider using fruit—a readily
available and inexpensive alternative to flowers.*

◀ CHRISTMAS CHEER

Red, green, and white are the colors of the season, and this stacked centerpiece shows them in a most refreshing way. For this design, fill a large bowl with floral foam. Use floral picks to secure apples into the foam around the edges of the bowl. Set a small bowl in the center of the large bowl and on top of the floral foam. Stack apples in the small bowl, and fill in the spaces with greenery and berry sprigs.

▲ ABUNDANTLY APPEALING

Fruits in a variety of glorious colors and shapes add richness to this filled-to-overflowing display. Pears, apples, oranges, grapes, figs, limes, star fruits, and persimmons are used here, but this idea works well with almost any combination. The container is filled with floral foam, and larger pieces of fruit are anchored into the foam using floral picks. Smaller fruits fill in the spaces. Bits of moss provide texture.

▲ SIMPLY DONE

A single row of pears in a flat, rectangular dish form an amazingly stylish table decoration. A touch of greenery softens the arrangement; otherwise, silky brown cording tied around the stems is the only adornment needed.

OLD WORLD CHARM

The holes in an antique sugar mold offer ideal receptacles for candles, fruits, and greenery. In lieu of a sugar mold, you can duplicate this arrangement using a rectangle of floral foam. Soak the floral foam in water, wrap it with chicken wire, and insert greenery and berries to cover the sides of the foam. Decorate the top with candles and an assortment of fruits and clippings. Use floral picks to secure the fruits into the foam. (To protect your tabletop, place the arrangement on a large platter or on plastic.) ▶

Sugar Mold Savvy

Sugar molds like the one pictured here can be found at antiques shops, but you may be surprised to learn that many home accessories stores carry reproductions, as well. See page 170 for sources.

GREENERY FROM THE GROCERY

Now that many large food stores have floral departments, you can shop for centerpieces while you shop for menu items. Here, we show ideas for arranging supermarket blooms in astonishing ways.

◀ WINTER WHITE

Combine paperwhites, poinsettias, maidenhair fern, and azaleas for an impressive green and white grouping. Simply place the plants in their individual pots into a more spacious and decorative container, such as this large silver bucket. First, line the container with a plastic bag. Then position the larger elements—paperwhites, poinsettias, and azaleas—and fill in the open spaces with maidenhair fern. For a denser look, remove the plants from their pots and plant them in the decorative container.

▲ CHANDELIER CENTERPIECE

To decorate a chandelier like this, you need a light fixture that has a flat base where potted plants can sit without sliding or falling through. Small pots of poinsettias and paperwhites, accented with variegated holly and greenery, are used here. If your chandelier isn't suited for this style arrangement, try the same grouping on a tabletop for an equally striking centerpiece. Here, a single ivy topiary becomes an attractive centerpiece when placed on a table runner and surrounded with angels and candles.

TOPIARY TREAT

For Christmas decoration and holiday gifts, consider the versatile live ivy topiary. Most grocery store floral departments carry these, but check the garden departments at home improvement centers and discount stores, as well.

Wound around a tree-shaped wire form, ivy makes a good backdrop or greenery filler in lots of seasonal arrangements. Place the topiary in its plastic pot into a decorative container for a delightfully quick gift. With the addition of wired ribbon and ornaments, it resembles a miniature Christmas tree. Once the holidays have passed, remove the embellishments, and the ivy carries on as a year-round houseplant.

HAT TRICK

The bright red flowers and rich green leaves of kalanchoe make it an appropriate selection for the Christmas season. Dress up the plastic pot by using a straw hat as a creative planter. An ideal gift for a garden enthusiast, the plant will be appreciated and the hat "container" will be welcomed sun protection for the gardener in the spring.

Set the plant in a plastic or cellophane bag to protect the inside of the hat, and then place the bag in the hat. Tie ribbon around the edge of the hat and around the plant.

POISED POINSETTIAS

Showcase poinsettia's vibrant color by clustering several together for impact. Partnered with red candles, these festive flowers shout Christmas. If the plant's foil-wrapped plastic pot doesn't suit your decor, remove the plant and set it in a moss-lined glass container. Be sure to place poinsettias in bright, but not direct, sunlight for at least six hours a day and keep the soil moist with lukewarm water. When selecting your plant, look for one with tightly clustered buds and no evidence of pollen on the leaves.

WRAPPED ARRANGEMENT

A gift package of roses and appleberry bush makes a sprightly holiday centerpiece or a present for a favorite friend. The red and green florals and the bright plaid ribbon are a delightfully festive combination.

To begin, place a water-soaked block of floral foam in a plastic bag and set it in the tin. Cut the stems of roses short and insert them into the foam. Fill in open spaces with appleberry bush or backyard greenery clippings. Wrap ribbon around the sides of the tin, securing it to the foam with wired floral picks. Fold a long piece of ribbon into loops, pinch it together in the center and secure it with a wired floral pick. Insert the pick into the floral foam at the center and fluff the loops.

CASUAL HOLIDAY MEALS

Count on serving company or your family
these stress-free holiday menus.

CHRISTMAS BREAKFAST

This festive morning meal includes everyone's favorites—eggs, sausage, biscuits, and fruit—in a delicious combination. The best feature is that much of the preparation can be done a day ahead.

MENU FOR 6 TO 8

Cream Cheese Scrambled Eggs

Sausage and Wild Rice Casserole

Ruby Pears • Cheese Biscuits

Banana Streusel Coffee Cake

Hot Percolator Punch

Ann Considine of Savannah, Georgia, and her family don't consider it Christmas until they've had "the breakfast." The Considines have been starting their Christmas celebration with this morning menu since 1981 when it first ran in *Southern Living® Annual Recipes.* "Our children are married now, but they come drifting back for the Christmas breakfast. The sausage casserole is our favorite," says Ann. Our Food staff recently retested and updated these recipes with today's tastes in mind to make them as dependable for your family as they have been for Ann's.

Here's a bountiful menu to start the Christmas day festivities. Pick only recipes that appeal to you, or take advantage of the make-ahead components and prepare them all. Get the family involved in making biscuits and stirring the eggs. The sausage casserole and Ruby Pears can be started the night before. Then they can bake side by side before the biscuits. While baking biscuits, let the punch perk. And if anyone's still hungry after the meal's under-way, a glazed coffee cake (that can be made a day ahead) awaits the sweet tooth.

CREAM CHEESE SCRAMBLED EGGS

Cream cheese and some gentle stirring produce creamy results for this skilletful of eggs.

12 large eggs
1   cup half-and-half or milk
2   (3-ounce) packages cream cheese, cubed
¾   teaspoon salt
¼   teaspoon pepper
¼   cup butter or margarine
Chopped fresh chives

  Process first 5 ingredients in a blender until frothy, stopping to scrape down sides.

  Melt butter in a large heavy skillet over medium heat; reduce heat to medium-low. Add egg mixture, and cook, without stirring, until mixture begins to set on bottom. Draw a spatula across bottom of skillet to form large curds. Continue cooking until eggs are thickened but still moist; do not stir constantly. Sprinkle with chives. Yield: 6 to 8 servings.

Stirring eggs only a few times during cooking pro-duces large, creamy curds.

SAUSAGE AND WILD RICE CASSEROLE

This meaty casserole topped with toasted nuts makes a hearty contribution to breakfast.

1   (6-ounce) package long-grain and wild rice mix (we tested with Uncle Ben's)
1   pound hot ground pork sausage
1   pound ground beef
1   large onion, chopped
1   (8-ounce) package sliced fresh mushrooms
1   (8-ounce) can sliced water chestnuts, drained
⅓   cup chopped fresh parsley
3   tablespoons soy sauce
1   (2.25-ounce) package sliced natural almonds (½ cup)

  Cook rice mix according to package directions.

  Cook sausage and ground beef in a large skillet, stirring until it crumbles and is no longer pink. Drain and pat dry with paper towels. Cook onion and mushrooms in same skillet over medium heat 7 minutes or until tender, stir-ring occasionally.

  Combine rice, sausage and beef, onion and mush-rooms, water chestnuts, parsley, and soy sauce; stir well. Spoon mixture into an ungreased 13" x 9" baking dish. Cover and chill casserole overnight.

  Remove from refrigerator, and let stand at room tem-perature 30 minutes. Sprinkle with almonds. Bake, uncov-ered, at 350° for 40 minutes or until thoroughly heated. Yield: 8 to 10 servings.

Note: *You don't have to refrigerate the casserole overnight. Just spoon it into the baking dish and bake, uncovered, at 350° for 20 minutes or until heated.*

RUBY PEARS

Serve these easy pear halves warm or chilled. The sweet jelly glaze and dollop of thick cream topping are what make them so good.

2   (29-ounce) cans pear halves, drained
2   cups ginger ale
¼   cup fresh orange juice (about 1 orange)
2   tablespoons fresh lemon juice (about ½ lemon)
2   tablespoons butter or margarine, melted
½   teaspoon ground cinnamon, divided
1   (12-ounce) jar red currant jelly
Mock Devonshire Cream
Garnish: ground cinnamon

Cream Cheese Scrambled Eggs,
Ruby Pears, Cheese Biscuits,
Sausage and Wild Rice Casserole

Arrange pear halves, cut side up, in an ungreased 13" x 9" baking dish. Stir together ginger ale and next 3 ingredients. Pour ginger ale mixture over pears; sprinkle with ¼ teaspoon cinnamon. Cover and chill at least 3 hours or overnight.

Remove pears from refrigerator, and let stand at room temperature 30 minutes. Uncover and bake at 350° for 40 minutes.

Melt jelly in a small saucepan over low heat; stir in remaining ¼ teaspoon cinnamon and 3 tablespoons pan juices.

Remove pears from baking dish using a slotted spoon. Place pears in a serving dish; pour jelly mixture over pears. Serve with Mock Devonshire Cream. Garnish, if desired. Yield: 6 to 8 servings.

MOCK DEVONSHIRE CREAM

1   cup whipping cream
½   cup sour cream
2   tablespoons powdered sugar
1   teaspoon vanilla extract

Beat whipping cream at high speed with an electric mixer until soft peaks form; fold in sour cream, sugar, and vanilla. Yield: 2¾ cups.

Note: *Otherwise known as clotted cream, Devonshire cream is a specialty of Devonshire, England. It's made by heating rich, unpasteurized milk and, after cooling, removing the thickened cream that forms a top layer. In our version, sour cream mocks the thick texture of the real cream.*

Banana Streusel Coffee Cake
Hot Percolator Punch

CHEESE BISCUITS

A little mustard boosts the cheese flavor in these quick biscuits. Quick tip: Grate the cheese the night before.

2 cups self-rising flour
1 teaspoon dry mustard
6 tablespoons shortening
1 cup (4 ounces) shredded sharp Cheddar cheese
¾ cup buttermilk

Stir together flour and mustard; cut in shortening with a pastry blender until mixture is crumbly. Stir in cheese. Add buttermilk, stirring until dry ingredients are moistened. Turn dough out onto a lightly floured surface, and knead 3 or 4 times.

Roll dough to ¾" thickness; cut with a 2" biscuit cutter. Place biscuits on a lightly greased baking sheet.

Bake at 450° for 10 to 12 minutes or until lightly browned. Yield: 1 dozen.

BANANA STREUSEL COFFEE CAKE

The yummy streusel's on the inside of this moist banana Bundt cake.

1 cup butter or margarine, softened
1½ cups sugar
2 large eggs
3 mashed ripe bananas (about 1⅓ cups)
1 teaspoon vanilla extract
2¼ cups all-purpose flour
1½ teaspoons baking powder
½ teaspoon baking soda
⅛ teaspoon salt
1 (8-ounce) container sour cream
¾ cup chopped pecans
2 tablespoons sugar
1 teaspoon ground cinnamon
1½ cups sifted powdered sugar
1 to 1½ tablespoons water

Beat butter at medium speed with an electric mixer until creamy; gradually add 1½ cups sugar, beating well. Add eggs, 1 at a time, beating until blended after each addition. Stir in banana and vanilla.

Combine flour and next 3 ingredients; add to butter mixture alternately with sour cream, beginning and ending with flour mixture. Beat at low speed until blended after each addition.

Rings of Old

It's a Southern thing to showcase our silver treasures. Use your family heirloom napkin rings for special occasions. These antique rings are numbered.

Combine pecans, 2 tablespoons sugar, and cinnamon. Pour half of batter into a greased and floured 12-cup Bundt pan; sprinkle with pecan mixture. Pour remaining batter over pecan layer. Bake at 350° for 50 minutes or until a long wooden pick inserted in center comes out clean. Cool in pan on a wire rack 10 minutes; remove from pan, and cool on wire rack.

Combine powdered sugar and water, stirring until smooth. Spoon glaze over cooled cake. Yield: 1 (10") cake.

HOT PERCOLATOR PUNCH

Here's a classic Southern Living punch that sends an inviting cinnamon aroma throughout your house as it perks.

3 cups unsweetened pineapple juice
3 cups cranberry-apple juice drink
1 cup water
⅓ cup firmly packed light brown sugar
2 lemon slices
2 (4") cinnamon sticks, broken
1½ teaspoons whole cloves
Cinnamon sticks (optional)

Pour juices and water into a 12-cup percolator. Place brown sugar and next 3 ingredients in percolator basket. Perk through complete cycle of electric percolator. Serve with cinnamon sticks, if desired. Yield: 7 cups.

Note: *This is an easy recipe to double if you have a larger percolator and a bigger crowd to serve.*

COUNTRY CHRISTMAS

Bring the mouthwatering goodness of country cooking back home.
This Old South menu is sure to remind family and friends of the pleasure found
in gathering for a holiday celebration filled with old-fashioned flavor.

MENU FOR 8

Brown Sugar Honey-Crusted Ham

Country Corn Relish

Homestyle Green Beans • Candied Sweet Potatoes and Apples

Biscuits or Rolls

Orange Pound Cake with Fresh Orange Syrup

Brown Sugar Honey-Crusted Ham,
Country Corn Relish, Homestyle
Green Beans, Candied Sweet
Potatoes and Apples

BROWN SUGAR HONEY-CRUSTED HAM

The sugar-crusted edge of baked ham is the best bite. This ham gets an extra sweet hit from honey.

1   (8-pound) smoked ham half (shank end)
⅔   cup honey
1   cup firmly packed light brown sugar
2   teaspoons ground nutmeg
1   teaspoon ground cloves
1   teaspoon ground cinnamon
Garnishes: lady apples and kumquats

Remove skin and excess fat from ham. Place ham, fat side up, on a rack in a shallow roasting pan lined with heavy-duty aluminum foil.

Bake, uncovered, at 325° for 1 hour and 15 minutes. Remove from oven.

Brush honey all over ham. Combine brown sugar and next 3 ingredients; pat sugar mixture over honey, coating ham thoroughly. Bake, uncovered, for 1 more hour or until a meat thermometer inserted into thickest part of ham registers 140°. Remove to a serving platter. Garnish, if desired. Yield: 12 to 14 servings.

COUNTRY CORN RELISH

This refrigerator relish makes enough for you to enjoy and to give away a few jars as gifts. The relish is almost as good without tomatoes, if you can't find good produce in the winter.

2   (15¼-ounce) cans whole kernel corn, drained
4   green onions, thinly sliced
4   plum tomatoes, diced
1   medium-size green bell pepper, diced
⅓   cup vegetable oil
⅓   cup apple cider vinegar
1   tablespoon sugar
½   teaspoon dried basil
½   teaspoon dried parsley flakes
¼   teaspoon dried crushed red pepper

Stir together first 4 ingredients in a large bowl.

Whisk together oil and remaining 5 ingredients. Pour oil mixture over corn mixture, and stir gently to combine. Cover and chill least 3 hours. Yield: 6 cups.

Colorful Country Corn Relish makes a great gift at Christmas or anytime.

Candied Sweet Potatoes and Apples

HOMESTYLE GREEN BEANS

You can't beat old-fashioned green beans for a simple side dish that suits the whole family.

2   pounds fresh green beans, trimmed and cut into
     1½" pieces
2   cups water
1   teaspoon salt
⅓   cup butter or margarine
1½ tablespoons sugar
1   teaspoon dried basil
½   teaspoon garlic powder
¼   teaspoon salt
¼   teaspoon pepper
2   cups halved cherry or grape tomatoes

Place beans in a Dutch oven; add water and salt. Bring to a boil; cover, reduce heat, and simmer 15 minutes or until tender. Drain; keep warm.

Melt butter in a saucepan over medium heat; stir in sugar and next 4 ingredients. Add tomato, and cook, stirring gently until thoroughly heated. Pour tomato mixture over beans, and toss gently. Serve hot. Yield: 8 servings.

CANDIED SWEET POTATOES AND APPLES

Prepare these candied vegetables a day ahead and chill them; then when the ham's finished baking, reheat the vegetables just before serving.

2   pounds sweet potatoes, peeled
1   cup firmly packed light brown sugar
1   cup butter or margarine
½   cup apple cider
¼   teaspoon salt
1   teaspoon vanilla extract
3   large Braeburn or other cooking apples, cored and
     cut into ½" rings

Cut sweet potatoes in half crosswise. Cook in boiling water to cover 10 minutes. Drain and cool. Cut crosswise into ½" slices.

Combine brown sugar and next 3 ingredients in a medium saucepan. Bring to a boil; boil 10 minutes. Remove from heat; stir in vanilla.

Layer sweet potato and apple slices in a greased 13" x 9" baking dish. Pour glaze over slices. Bake, uncovered, at 400° for 1 hour or until potatoes are candied and glaze is thickened, basting with glaze after 30 minutes. Yield: 8 servings.

ORANGE POUND CAKE WITH FRESH ORANGE SYRUP

Pound cake is the Southern dessert for all occasions. This orange-scented version makes a nice finish for the holiday meal.

1   cup butter, softened
2   cups sugar
4   large eggs
3   cups all-purpose flour
½   teaspoon baking soda
⅛   teaspoon salt
1   cup buttermilk
2   teaspoons orange extract
1   teaspoon vanilla extract
Powdered Sugar
Fresh Orange Syrup

Beat butter at medium speed with an electric mixer about 2 minutes or until creamy. Gradually add sugar, beating 5 to 7 minutes. Add eggs, 1 at a time, beating just until yellow disappears.

Combine flour, baking soda, and salt; add to butter mixture alternately with buttermilk, beginning and ending with flour mixture. Beat at low speed just until blended after each addition. Stir in flavorings. Pour batter into a greased and floured 10" tube pan.

Bake at 350° for 55 minutes or until a long wooden pick inserted in center comes out clean. Cool in pan on a wire rack 10 to 15 minutes; remove from pan, and cool on wire rack. Sprinkle with powdered sugar. Serve with Fresh Orange Syrup. Yield: 1 (10") cake.

FRESH ORANGE SYRUP

1⅓   cups fresh orange juice (about 6 oranges)
1   cup sugar
1   tablespoon butter
1⅓   cups fresh orange sections (about 3 oranges)

Combine orange juice and sugar in a large nonaluminum skillet. Bring to a boil over medium heat, stirring constantly until sugar dissolves. Cook 17 minutes or until mixture is reduced to 1 cup. Remove from heat; add butter, stirring until butter melts. Gently stir in orange sections. Serve warm, or cover and chill. Stir gently just before serving. Store in an airtight container in refrigerator. Yield: 2 cups.

CAROLERS' WARM-UP

While caroling warms hearts, this robust menu satisfies appetites.
Get started on the right note with mugs of Hot Spiced Wine for adults and hot cocoa
for the children. Then serve filling chili and savory scones (make a double batch
if your crowd is large), and be sure everyone grabs a crackle
cookie as they head out the door.

MENU FOR 6

Hot Spiced Wine • Hot cocoa

Thick Three-Bean Chili

Cheddar Scones

Spicy Chocolate Crackles

HOT SPICED WINE

A quick version of mulled wine, this party drink highlights a
wonderful blend of spice and citrus.

2   (3") cinnamon sticks
2   teaspoons whole cloves
1   teaspoon whole allspice
6   cups fruity red wine (such as Beaujolais or
     Pinot Noir)
6   cups apple cider
¾   cup sugar
1   orange, thinly sliced
1   lemon, thinly sliced
1   lime, thinly sliced

   Place first 3 ingredients on an 8" square of cheesecloth;
tie with string. Place spice bag in a Dutch oven. Add red
wine and remaining 5 ingredients; bring to a simmer over
low heat (do not boil). Keep at a simmer while serving.
Ladle into mugs. Yield: 13 cups.

Note: *For a nonalcoholic version, omit wine and substitute*
more apple cider.

THICK THREE-BEAN CHILI

We liked the three beans used here, but you could use all
kidney beans if you prefer.

1   pound ground round
1   medium onion, chopped
2   jalapeño peppers, seeded and chopped
2   tablespoons chili powder
2   teaspoons brown sugar
½   teaspoon ground red pepper
¼   teaspoon ground cumin
2   (15-ounce) cans tomato sauce
1   (6-ounce) can tomato paste
1¾ cups water
1¼ cups beer or beef broth
1   teaspoon apple cider vinegar
1   (16-ounce) can light red kidney beans, drained
1   (15.5-ounce) can butter beans, drained
1   (15-ounce) can chickpeas, drained
½   teaspoon salt

   Cook ground round and onion in a Dutch oven over
medium-high heat, stirring until meat crumbles and onion
is tender; drain. Return to pan.
   Add jalapeño pepper and next 4 ingredients; cook 2
minutes. Add tomato sauce and next 4 ingredients; stir
well. Stir in beans. Bring to a boil; reduce heat, and simmer, uncovered, over medium-low heat 45 minutes, stirring
occasionally. Stir in salt before serving. Yield: about 11 cups.

Thick Three-Bean Chili
Cheddar Scone

Cheddar Scones

SPICY CHOCOLATE CRACKLES

Ground ginger and pepper (yes, pepper) spice up this sugar-coated cookie kids will like.

1   (18.25-ounce) package devil's food cake mix
⅓   cup vegetable oil
2   large eggs, lightly beaten
1   tablespoon ground ginger
½   teaspoon ground pepper
1   tablespoon water
½   cup semisweet chocolate mini-morsels
¼   cup sugar

Combine first 6 ingredients in a large bowl, stirring until smooth. Stir in mini-morsels.

Shape dough into 1" balls; roll in sugar to coat. Place balls 2" apart on lightly greased baking sheets.

Bake at 375° for 9 minutes. Cool 2 to 3 minutes on baking sheets. Remove to wire racks to cool completely. Yield: 4 dozen.

CHEDDAR SCONES

These light-textured little wedges of cheese bread are ideal for dunking into a steaming bowl of chili. They're also good for breakfast.

1¾ cups all-purpose flour
1   tablespoon sugar
2   teaspoons baking powder
¾   teaspoon salt
¼   cup cold butter, cut into pieces
1   cup (4 ounces) finely shredded sharp Cheddar cheese
1   large egg, lightly beaten
⅔   cup half-and-half
1   tablespoon butter, melted

Combine first 4 ingredients in a large bowl; cut in cold butter with a pastry blender until mixture is crumbly. Stir in cheese.

Stir together egg and half-and-half. Gradually add to flour mixture, stirring with a fork just until dry ingredients are moistened. Turn dough out onto a lightly floured surface, and knead 3 or 4 times. Gently roll into a ball.

Pat dough into a 7" circle on an ungreased baking sheet. Cut into 6 wedges, using a sharp knife. (Do not separate wedges.)

Bake at 400° for 16 to 18 minutes or until golden. Remove from oven; brush with 1 tablespoon melted butter. Serve warm. Yield: 6 scones.

Hot Spiced Wine, hot cocoa, Spicy Chocolate Crackles

Manicotti Night

*Manicotti is a filling main dish, one you can make ahead and
count on for company. This rich meatless version partners well with a beautiful,
fresh green salad. And the dessert's easy—make the cookies ahead and
pick up some sorbet at the market.*

Menu for 6

Field Greens with Tangerine Dressing and Pesto Wafers

Shiitake Mushroom and Spinach Manicotti • Pistachio Shortbread Crisps

Field Greens with Tangerine Dressing

FIELD GREENS WITH TANGERINE DRESSING AND PESTO WAFERS

A lively citrus dressing and some crisp cheese wafers adorn this bowl of greens.

⅓ cup loosely packed fresh basil leaves
2 tablespoons pine nuts
1 garlic clove, halved
3 ounces freshly grated Parmigiano-Reggiano cheese
6 cups loosely packed gourmet mixed salad greens
Tangerine Dressing
3 tangerines, sectioned
½ small purple onion, halved and thinly sliced

Combine first 3 ingredients in a food processor or blender; process until smooth, stopping to scrape down sides. Stir together basil mixture and grated cheese in a small bowl.

Place a 1½" round cutter on a lightly greased baking sheet. Sprinkle 1 tablespoon cheese mixture into cutter.

Press cheese into cutter; remove cutter. Repeat procedure with remaining cheese mixture, spacing wafers 2" apart. Bake at 350° for 10 to 12 minutes or until edges are browned. Cool 30 seconds on baking sheet. Remove to wire racks to cool completely.

Toss salad greens with Tangerine Dressing. Add tangerine sections and onion slices. Serve with cheese wafers. Yield: 6 servings.

TANGERINE DRESSING

⅓ cup fresh tangerine juice (about 2 large tangerines)
2 tablespoons extra-virgin olive oil
1 tablespoon white wine vinegar
1 tablespoon honey
2 teaspoons minced shallot
¼ teaspoon salt

Whisk together all ingredients. Yield: ½ cup.

Going, Going, Gone

These thin, crisp pesto wafers may just be the highlight of the meal. (They're part of the salad recipe.) You won't be able to stop at just one.

SHIITAKE MUSHROOM AND SPINACH MANICOTTI

This creamy, crusty-topped casserole is a great make-ahead option for the holiday rush.

12   manicotti or cannelloni shells
¼   cup butter or margarine, divided
4½   cups sliced fresh shiitake or other mushrooms (8 ounces)
2   garlic cloves, minced
1   (10-ounce) package fresh spinach, coarse stems removed
1   cup ricotta cheese
3   ounces freshly grated Parmesan cheese
1   large egg, beaten
½   teaspoon salt
½   teaspoon freshly ground pepper
⅓   cup butter or margarine
2   tablespoons all-purpose flour
2   cups half-and-half
½   teaspoon salt
1   cup (4 ounces) shredded Gouda cheese
2   7-grain sandwich bread slices (we tested with Branola)
1½   cups (6 ounces) shredded Mexican four-cheese blend
3   tablespoons butter or margarine, melted

Cook shells according to package directions; drain.

Meanwhile, melt 3 tablespoons butter in a large skillet; add mushrooms and garlic, and sauté until mushroom liquid is absorbed. Transfer mushroom mixture to a large bowl.

Melt remaining 1 tablespoon butter in skillet. Add spinach; cover and cook over medium-low heat 5 minutes or until spinach wilts. Add spinach to mushroom mixture. Stir in ricotta cheese and next 4 ingredients. Spoon spinach mixture evenly into shells. Place stuffed shells in a greased 13" x 9" baking dish.

Melt ⅓ cup butter in a heavy saucepan over low heat; whisk in flour until smooth. Cook 1 minute, whisking constantly. Gradually whisk in half-and-half; cook over medium heat, whisking constantly, until mixture is thickened and bubbly. Stir in ½ teaspoon salt. Add Gouda cheese, stirring until cheese melts. Pour over stuffed shells.

Process bread in a blender or food processor until it resembles coarse crumbs. Spread crumbs in a small pan; bake at 350° for 3 to 4 minutes or until toasted. Combine toasted crumbs, cheese blend, and 3 tablespoons melted butter in a bowl; toss well, and sprinkle over shells.

Bake, uncovered, at 350° for 45 minutes or until bubbly. Yield: 6 servings.

Note: *If desired, cover and chill manicotti at least 8 hours before baking. Remove from refrigerator, and let stand at room temperature 30 minutes. Bake as directed.*

PISTACHIO SHORTBREAD CRISPS

Serve these thick, crisp, nutty cookies with lemon sorbet or vanilla ice cream.

1   cup butter, softened
½   cup sugar
2   teaspoons vanilla extract
2   cups all-purpose flour
1   cup pistachio nuts
Sugar

Beat butter at medium speed with an electric mixer until creamy; gradually add ½ cup sugar, beating well. Add vanilla, beating until blended. Gradually add flour, beating just until combined.

Process pistachios in a food processor until coarsely ground. Place ground nuts on a plate.

Shape dough into 1" balls. Working over plate of nuts with 1 ball at a time, sprinkle about 1 tablespoon nuts over ball, pressing nuts gently into ball. Repeat procedure with remaining balls and nuts. Place balls on ungreased baking sheets; flatten to ⅜" thickness. Sprinkle with sugar.

Bake at 350° for 10 minutes or until lightly browned. Immediately remove to wire racks to cool completely. Yield: about 2½ dozen.

COCKTAIL HOUR

Set out an assortment of these Mediterranean-inspired hors d'oeuvres along with your favorite wines, cheeses, and fruit, and you've got a holiday happy hour ready and waiting. Both relishes and pita toasts can be made ahead.

MENU FOR 12 OR MORE

Roasted Onions, Figs, and Smoked Sausage

Kalamata Olive Relish • Green Olive Relish

Toasted Pita Wedges

Walnut-Basil Pastries with Dried Tomatoes

Prosciutto Crab Cakes with Red Pepper Mayonnaise

Assorted fruit and cheeses

Red and white wines

Fruit and Cheese Tray

Embellish this party spread with red and green grapes, crisp apples and pears, a combination of hard and soft cheeses, some nuts, and breadsticks.

Roasted Onions, Figs, and Smoked Sausage

ROASTED ONIONS, FIGS, AND SMOKED SAUSAGE

This serving bowl holds a roasted antipasto option. Set out forks for your guests.

1   (8-ounce) package dried figs, quartered
½   cup apricot nectar
¼   cup honey
2   tablespoons balsamic vinegar
1   teaspoon chopped fresh rosemary
1   pound kielbasa or other smoked sausage, cut into ½" slices
2   cups coarsely chopped onion
2   small sweet potatoes, peeled and cut into 1" pieces (about 2½ cups)

Combine first 3 ingredients in a small saucepan. Bring to a boil; cover and cook 1 minute. Remove from heat, and let stand 30 minutes. Stir in vinegar and rosemary; set aside.

Combine sausage, onion, and sweet potato in a large greased roasting pan. Bake, uncovered, at 450° for 30 minutes, stirring occasionally.

Stir fig mixture into sausage mixture; bake 10 more minutes. Serve warm or at room temperature. Yield: 12 appetizer servings.

KALAMATA OLIVE RELISH

This relish has a chunky texture thanks to whole nuts and olives chopped by hand.

2   tablespoons pine nuts
¼   cup dried tomatoes in oil, undrained
½   cup minced onion
1   tablespoon minced garlic
2   teaspoons dried basil
1   (8-ounce) jar kalamata olives, drained, pitted, and chopped

Bake nuts in a shallow pan at 350°, stirring occasionally, 5 minutes or until toasted. Drain dried tomatoes, reserving 2 tablespoons oil. Coarsely chop tomatoes.

Sauté onion in reserved oil in a large skillet over medium-high heat 5 minutes or until tender. Add garlic and sauté 1 minute. Add tomato and basil. Process tomato mixture in a blender or food processor 5 seconds or until almost pureed; place in a small bowl. Stir in olives and pine nuts. Cover and chill relish up to 1 week. Serve relish at room temperature. Yield: 2 cups.

GREEN OLIVE RELISH

All the ingredients for this relish are blended in a food processor, producing a fine-textured finish.

2   garlic cloves
1   (7-ounce) jar pimiento-stuffed olives, drained
⅓   cup chopped fresh parsley
2   tablespoons olive oil
2   teaspoons lemon juice
1   teaspoon anchovy paste

Process garlic in a food processor until minced. Add olives and remaining ingredients; process until olives are finely chopped. Cover and chill relish up to 1 week. Serve relish at room temperature. Yield: 1¼ cups.

TOASTED PITA WEDGES

3   (6") pita bread rounds, split
Olive oil-flavored cooking spray

Cut each bread half into 8 wedges.

Place wedges in a single layer on an ungreased baking sheet; spray lightly with cooking spray. Bake at 350° for 6 to 8 minutes or until crisp. Yield: 4 dozen.

Kalamata Olive Relish
Green Olive Relish
Toasted Pita Wedges

WALNUT-BASIL PASTRIES WITH DRIED TOMATOES

Savory Mediterranean flavors fill these flaky pastry triangles.

16 frozen 14"-x 18" phyllo pastry sheets, thawed in refrigerator
¾ cup butter, melted
8   (1-ounce) slices provolone cheese, quartered
Walnut-Ricotta Spread
14 dried tomatoes in oil, drained and coarsely chopped
Garnish: fresh basil sprigs

Place 2 sheets of phyllo on a work surface (keeping remaining phyllo covered). Brush top sheet with melted butter. Cut buttered phyllo sheets lengthwise into 4 equal strips (about 3½" wide). Place 1 piece of provolone (folded, if necessary) onto 1 end of each strip. Spoon a scant tablespoon of Walnut-Ricotta Spread over cheese; top with a few pieces of dried tomato.

Working with 1 strip at a time, fold bottom corner of phyllo over filling, forming a triangle. Continue folding back and forth to end of strip. Lightly brush phyllo triangle with butter to seal. Repeat procedure with remaining phyllo (2 sheets at a time), butter, provolone, Walnut-Ricotta Spread, and dried tomatoes.

Place pastries on an ungreased baking sheet. Bake at 425° for 10 to 11 minutes or until evenly browned. Serve warm or at room temperature. Garnish, if desired. Yield: 32 pastries.

WALNUT-RICOTTA SPREAD

2   small garlic cloves
1   cup ricotta cheese
¾   cup grated Parmesan cheese
1   teaspoon sugar
½   cup chopped walnuts
12 fresh basil leaves, sliced
1   tablespoon olive oil
½   teaspoon salt
¼   teaspoon pepper

With food processor running, drop garlic cloves through food chute; process until minced. Add cheeses and sugar; process until smooth, stopping to scrape down sides. Add walnuts, basil, olive oil, salt, and pepper; process until blended. Yield: 1½ cups.

Walnut-Basil Pastries with Dried Tomatoes

Prosciutto Crab Cakes with Red Pepper Mayonnaise

Prosciutto Crab Cakes with Red Pepper Mayonnaise

Prosciutto (salt-cured Italian ham) is a nice surprise in these meaty cakes. Country ham makes a suitable substitute.

1   pound fresh lump crabmeat, drained
½   cup shaved prosciutto, finely chopped
½   cup French breadcrumbs (homemade)
1   large egg, lightly beaten
2   tablespoons grated onion
2   teaspoons white wine Worcestershire sauce
½   teaspoon salt
2   tablespoons butter or margarine, melted
2   tablespoons vegetable oil
Red Pepper Mayonnaise
Garnish: lemon slices

Combine crabmeat, prosciutto, and breadcrumbs in a bowl. Toss gently.

Stir together egg and next 3 ingredients in a small bowl. Gently fold egg mixture into crabmeat. Cover and chill at least ½ hour. Shape mixture into 12 patties, using a scant ¼ cupful for each. Place patties on a wax paper-lined baking sheet; cover and chill at least 1 hour.

Cook 6 patties in 1 tablespoon butter and 1 tablespoon oil in a large nonstick skillet over medium-high heat 5 to 6 minutes on each side or until browned. Remove from skillet; set aside, and keep warm. Repeat procedure with remaining patties, butter, and oil. Serve warm with Red Pepper Mayonnaise. Garnish, if desired. Yield: 12 crab cakes.

Red Pepper Mayonnaise

2   garlic cloves
⅓   cup drained and diced roasted sweet red peppers
½   teaspoon fresh lemon juice
⅛   teaspoon ground red pepper
1   cup mayonnaise, divided

With food processor running, drop garlic through food chute. Add diced pepper, lemon juice, ground pepper, and ¼ cup mayonnaise. Process 1 minute or until very smooth, stopping to scrape down sides. Transfer to a bowl; stir in remaining ¾ cup mayonnaise. Cover and chill at least 8 hours. Yield: 1⅓ cups.

WINTER HARVEST SUPPER

Savor the holiday season with a celebration featuring nature's bountiful food gifts. Begin the feast with ginger-kissed bowls of butternut soup. Then feast on a platter of mustard-crusted pork and roasted potatoes. Decorate each plate with glistening cranapple sauce. And for dessert, offer our dressed-up apple pie.

MENU FOR 6 TO 8

Butternut Squash Soup

Mustard-Crusted Pork Roast and Browned Potatoes

Cinnamon-Scented Cranapple Sauce

Green Bean Casserole with Fried Leeks

Dinner rolls

Cornmeal Streusel Apple Pie

Mustard-Crusted Pork Roast and Browned Potatoes

BUTTERNUT SQUASH SOUP

This velvety starter soup is a blend of pureed squash and carrots, cream, and a hint of ginger.

1   (3-pound) butternut squash
¾   pound carrots, scraped and cut into chunks
      (8 carrots)
2½ cups chicken broth
¾   cup orange juice
½   teaspoon salt
½   teaspoon ground ginger
½   cup whipping cream
2   tablespoons finely chopped pecans, toasted
Ground nutmeg

Cut squash in half lengthwise; remove seeds. Place squash, cut sides down, in a shallow pan; add hot water to pan to depth of ¾". Cover with aluminum foil, and bake at 400° for 40 minutes or until tender; drain. Scoop out pulp; mash. Discard shell. Cook carrot in boiling water 25 minutes or until tender; drain and mash.

Combine squash, carrot, chicken broth, and next 3 ingredients in a bowl. Process half of mixture in a food processor or blender until smooth. Repeat procedure with remaining half of squash mixture.

Place pureed mixture in a large saucepan; bring to a simmer. Stir in cream; return to a simmer. Remove from heat. To serve, ladle into individual bowls. Sprinkle with pecans and nutmeg. Yield: 8 cups.

MUSTARD-CRUSTED PORK ROAST AND BROWNED POTATOES

A mustardy glaze locks moisture in this pork roast. Rosemary potatoes roast alongside the pork, making a rustic side dish.

1   (4-to 5-pound) boneless pork loin roast
¼   teaspoon salt
¼   teaspoon pepper
½   cup coarse-grained mustard
8   garlic cloves, minced
3   tablespoons olive oil
3   tablespoons balsamic vinegar
2   tablespoons chopped fresh rosemary
2   pounds new potatoes
2   tablespoons olive oil
1   tablespoon chopped fresh rosemary
½   teaspoon salt
½   teaspoon pepper
Garnish: fresh rosemary sprigs

Place pork in a greased roasting pan. Rub with ¼ teaspoon each salt and pepper. Combine mustard and next 4 ingredients in a small bowl; spread evenly over pork.

Peel a crosswise stripe around each potato with a vegetable peeler, if desired. Cut each potato in half lengthwise. Toss potatoes with 2 tablespoons oil, 1 tablespoon chopped rosemary, ½ teaspoon salt, and ½ teaspoon pepper. Add to roasting pan around pork. Insert meat thermometer into thickest part of roast.

Bake at 375° for 1 hour to 1¼ hours or until thermometer registers 160°. Let stand 10 minutes. Transfer roast to a serving platter. Surround pork with potatoes. Garnish, if desired. Yield: 8 servings.

CINNAMON-SCENTED CRANAPPLE SAUCE

This jewel-toned cranberry sauce gets embellished with tart apple, cinnamon pears, and citrus. It's a wonderful match for pork roast or turkey.

1   (16-ounce) can whole-berry cranberry sauce
1   (15-ounce) can cinnamon-flavored pear halves, drained and chopped
1   (11-ounce) can mandarin orange segments, drained
1   Granny Smith apple, peeled and chopped
1   cup sugar
½   cup dried fruit mix (we tested with Mariani Harvest Medley)

Cinnamon-Scented Cranapple Sauce

Combine all ingredients in a large saucepan; cook, uncovered, over medium-low heat 45 minutes or until thickened, stirring often. Remove sauce from heat; cover and chill.

Serve as an accompaniment to pork or turkey, or as a topping over vanilla ice cream, pound cake, or pancakes. Yield: 3½ cups.

Note: *If you can't find cinnamon-flavored pears, use regular canned pear halves and add ½ teaspoon ground cinnamon.*

Mustard-Crusted Pork Roast and Browned Potatoes,
Cinnamon-Scented Cranapple Sauce,
Green Bean Casserole with Fried Leeks

GREEN BEAN CASSEROLE WITH FRIED LEEKS

Remember the old green bean casserole made with convenience products: frozen or canned green beans, cream of mushroom soup, and French fried onions? Here it is again, only updated with some upscale ingredients.

2   tablespoons butter or margarine
2   (8-ounce) packages sliced fresh mushrooms
1   teaspoon dried thyme
2   shallots, finely chopped
½   cup Madeira
1   cup whipping cream
1¼ pounds fresh green beans, trimmed
Vegetable or peanut oil
2   large leeks, cleaned and thinly sliced crosswise
Salt

Melt butter in large heavy skillet over medium-high heat. Add mushrooms and thyme; sauté 5 minutes. Add shallots; sauté 3 minutes or until tender. Add Madeira, and cook over medium-high heat 3 minutes or until liquid evaporates. Add whipping cream, and cook 2 to 5 minutes or until slightly thickened. Remove from heat.

Meanwhile, cook beans in a small amount of boiling water 5 minutes or just until crisp-tender; drain. Add beans to mushroom mixture, and toss gently. Spoon into a greased 2-quart gratin dish or shallow baking dish. Cover and keep warm.

Pour oil to depth of 2" into a 3-quart saucepan; heat to 350°. Fry leeks in 3 batches, 40 seconds or until golden. Remove leeks with small metal strainer; drain on paper towels. Immediately sprinkle with salt. Sprinkle fried leeks over warm bean mixture. Bake, uncovered, at 400° for 5 minutes or until casserole is thoroughly heated. Yield: 6 servings.